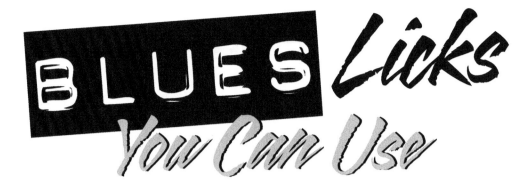

MUSIC AND PERFORMANCE NOTES
FOR 75 HOT LEAD PHRASES

PLAYBACK+
Speed • Pitch • Balance • Loop

To access audio visit:
www.halleonard.com/mylibrary

Enter Code
4330-6104-4764-4721

Other Hal Leonard books by John Ganapes:

Blues You Can Use
HL00695007

More Blues You Can Use
HL00695165

Blues You Can Use Guitar Chords
HL00695082

T0048529

ISBN 978-0-634-00829-0

7777 W. BLUEMOUND RD. P.O. BOX 13819 MILWAUKEE, WI 53213

Visit Hal Leonard Online at
www.halleonard.com

TABLE OF CONTENTS

All music composed and arranged by John Ganapes.

Produced by John Ganapes and Walter Chancellor, Jr..

Recorded at Electronic Musicians Workshop, EMW Records, Minneapolis, MN.

And at Jungle Rootz Productions, Minneapolis, MN; Echo Martin: Engineer

Musicians:

John Ganapes — guitar

Tom Tange — keyboards

David Harris — bass

Jason Santa Lucia — drums

*all guitar parts were played using a *Line-6 Pod* and *Pod Pro* ™
(the setting used can be found in the Tone-Transfer area of www.line6.com)

INTRODUCTION

Who Can Use This Book

The purpose of *Blues Licks You Can Use* is to give aspiring blues guitarists and experienced players alike a large chunk of the vocabulary of the blues — in other words, *lots of licks.*

While it is not necessary to have tremendous technique to begin working in this book, you need to be able to make your fingers do what you want them to. In fact, learning the licks contained inside will help you to develop your technique. As you progress through the book, however, the licks become more difficult and some require a great deal of technical ability to perform. Don't let the difficult licks discourage you. Just keep working on them; you'll have them under your fingers before too long. If you don't feel you have the skills necessary to learn the material in this book, I suggest that you work through the two core books in this series—*Blues You Can Use* and *More Blues You Can Use.* Mastering the material in these two will allow you to tackle anything you find in this book.

There are some things you should know. You need to know the Minor Pentatonic and Major Pentatonic scales as well as the blues scales. You should know them over the entire fingerboard, in every position, and in every key. You should also know the basic chords used in the blues—at least two or three different voicings (shapes) each of major and minor chords, seventh chords, ninth chords, and minor seventh chords. More is better. A basic knowledge of the 12-bar blues progression is essential.

Even if you don't know all or much of the above, you can still benefit from working through this book. You just won't understand very well how the licks are working, or where they come from. It will be much more difficult, though not impossible, to take what is contained in this book and apply it to your own personal style. You need at least a basic understanding of theory and the layout of the guitar to do that.

Look at the *Review of the Materials Used in the Book* later in this section to see graphically what you should know.

Blues You Can Use and *More Blues You Can Use* will give you a thorough knowledge of the blues and fill in any gaps you might have. I strongly suggest that you work through them if you don't already have a command of those materials.

How to Use This Book

These are real licks. They're played by real blues guitarists—each in his own way. While you will no doubt recognize some of the styles contained in this book, a great effort was made to keep the licks "generic" and not exactly as each specific blues great played them. Albert King and Stevie Ray Vaughan might both have used the same lick in this book, but the exact performance of that lick would be different as each individual guitarist played it. Once you have learned a lick, you should listen for it on various recordings to hear how the various masters played them. Blues guitar styles have evolved through new players borrowing material from past masters and putting their own twists on it.

Learn each lick slowly at first, gradually building up speed. Never play a lick faster than you can control. If a lick gets sloppy, slow it down. Once you have learned a lick as written, try playing it in different positions and scale patterns. Play it everywhere you can find it on the fingerboard. Then, transpose it to every key. By working through them this way, you'll learn the fingerboard better and know how to use each lick in any tune it fits.

The following example illustrates how to go about learning the licks everywhere you can find them in a given key. After you have worked a lick in this way, do the same in all of the other keys.

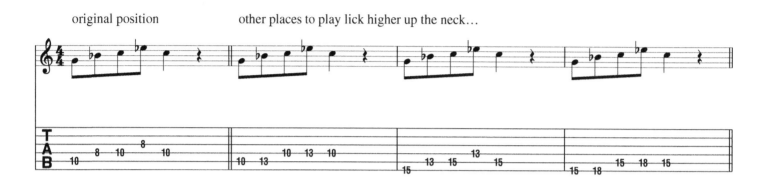

Audio Supplement

The audio contains all of the licks in this book—one to a track. First, the lick is played slowly (half-speed) and then at full tempo.

The second track contains tuning notes for all six strings so that you can play in tune with the audio.

Tracks 78-82 feature backing tracks. The five chord progressions in the book are played with a full band so that you can use the licks you learn in each section in your own solo. Each progression is played several times through. You should try using the licks from one section along with the progression of another. You'll gain valuable experience transposing the licks and changing the timing and feel to make them fit the new progression.

Review of the Materials Used in the Book

The following chords, scales, and patterns are used and discussed throughout the book and should be understood by the reader.

Major and minor pentatonic scales.

Pattern 1 – Minor
Pattern 5 – Major

Pattern 2 – Minor
Pattern 1 – Major

Pattern 3 – Minor
Pattern 2 – Major

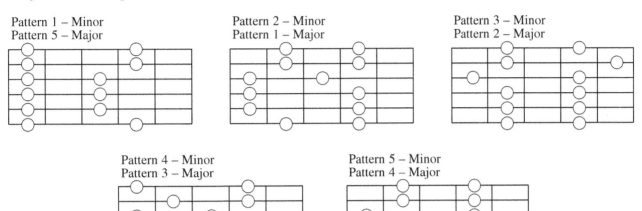

Pattern 4 – Minor
Pattern 3 – Major

Pattern 5 – Minor
Pattern 4 – Major

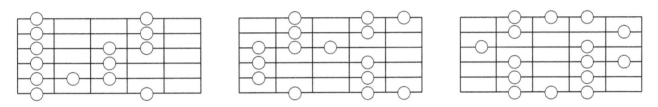

Blues scale—five patterns.

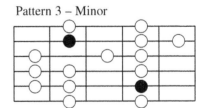
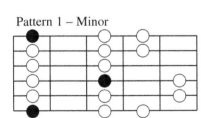

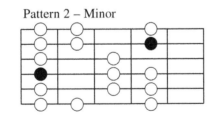

*Dorian mode—based on the five patterns of the minor pentatonic scale.

Pattern 1 – Minor

Pattern 2 – Minor

Pattern 3 – Minor

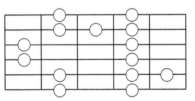
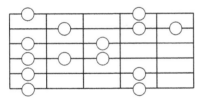

Pattern 4 – Minor

Pattern 5 – Minor

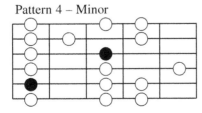
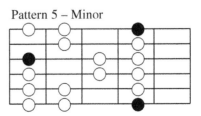

*Mixolydian mode — based on the five patterns of the major pentatonic scale.

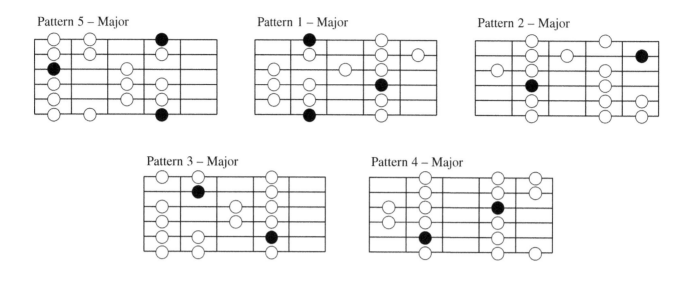

Pattern 5 – Major   Pattern 1 – Major   Pattern 2 – Major

Pattern 3 – Major   Pattern 4 – Major

Dominant seventh-type chord — notes up to the 9th of the chord.

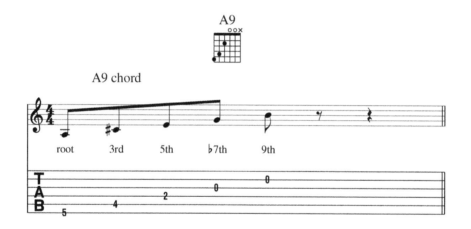

A9

A9 chord

root   3rd   5th   ♭7th   9th

*Don't worry if you've never heard of the Dorian and Mixolydian modes. They are very useful for more jazz-like blues, but you needn't know them well to get the most out of this book.

SECTION 1

GROOVIN' EASY: LICKS 1 - 15

Journeyman Licks and Tricks in the Key of C

This first section contains some shorter licks to help you get started. They're fairly easy to play and use in a slow blues, but don't get the impression that they are amateur licks—they're not. You can use these onstage with the best. In fact, some of the best blues players have used licks much like these in concert and on CD.

They are written in the key of C, using C7 (or C9) for the I chord, F7 (or F9) for the IV chord, and G7 (or G9) for the V. It's up to you to work them out in the other keys.

The licks presented in this book are made up of smaller fragments called *motives* or *melodic figures.* As you work through the book, you'll see that many of the licks are made up of the same motives—often changed slightly to fit the new lick or different chords.

If you find that transposing the complete lick is difficult, try taking the smaller motives or fragments of each lick and learning them first. You can use them in any way that sounds good to you. If you use them on the chords indicated, you'll certainly be "correct" in your usage of them. After you find the smaller motives, try putting the whole lick together in the new key. Remember: learn everything in every key if you want these licks to be useful to you.

These licks can all be used in a "quick-change" 12-bar blues tune using the chords given below. Let's take a look at the progression first. Listen to it a few times to get the sound of it in your head. You can hear the band play it on audio track 78.

78 **C Dominant 12-Bar Quickchange**

Slow Blues in C

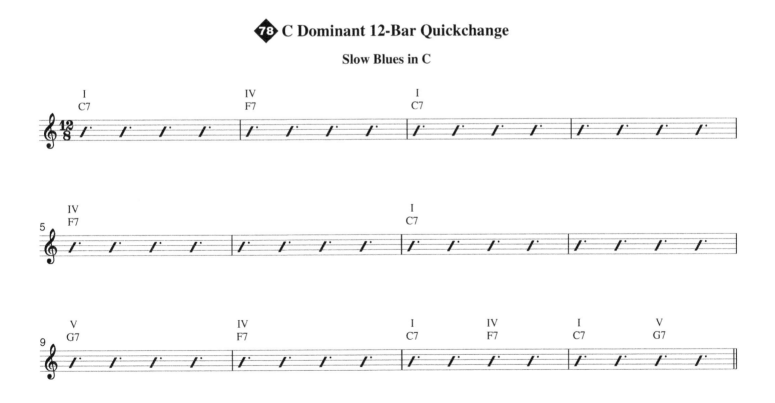

The first set of licks can be used in the opening four bars of the progression. *Licks 1, 2,* and *3* are all built from the C minor pentatonic scale. You'll notice that they are made up of many of the same motives. *Lick 3* is only two bars long and can be used anywhere you find a I chord followed by a IV. It will work in bars 4 and 5 as well as in bars 1 and 2.

3 ◆ Lick 1

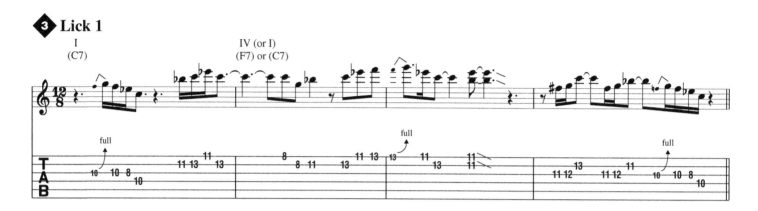

4 ◆ Lick 2

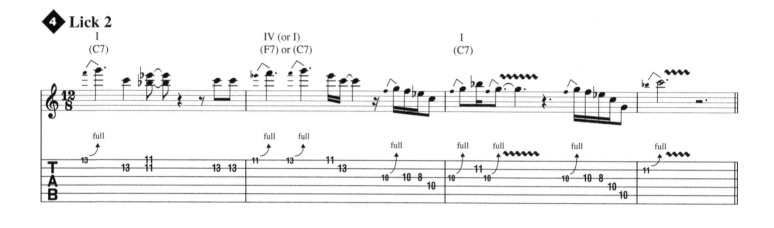

5 ◆ Lick 3

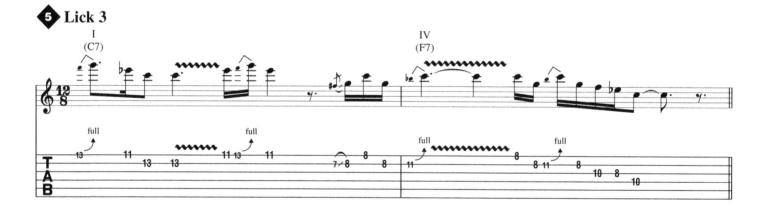

Lick 4 is built from both the C major pentatonic and the C minor pentatonic scales. It starts with the major in the first bar, shifts to the minor when you change to the IV chord in the second bar, and then returns to the major for the I chord in the pick-up to bar 3. It ends with notes from the minor pentatonic scale in the final bar (the 5th and ♭7th of the I chord) and a repeat of the string-bend figure into the IV chord.

Lick 5 is made up of notes taken from the minor pentatonic scale with a repeated triplet figure containing a passing note between the E♭ and F (the E♮ in the second full bar, played over the IV chord). You could play that figure alone in bars 5 and 6, where you have two bars of a IV chord.

◆6 Lick 4

◆7 Lick 5

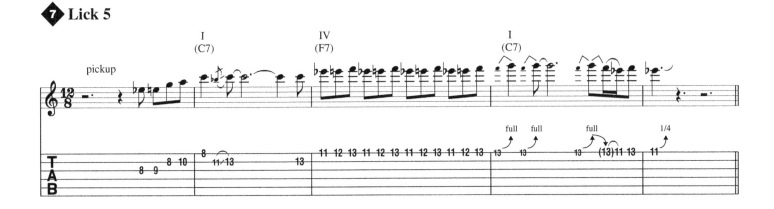

You can use the licks in their entirety, or as I mentioned above, you can take a smaller piece of a lick to play in one or two bars. Just be sure that you are using the lick fragment with the correct chord(s). For example, you can play the last bar of *Lick 1* by itself wherever a I chord appears in the tune. It wouldn't sound very good played over a IV chord though, and would sound even worse on a V chord.

After the first four bars of the progression, you come to a two-bar section of the IV chord. The following three licks (*6-8*) can be used there, or in any tune where you have two bars of a IV7 chord. Remember: these licks can be used in any tune where you want a bluesy sound—not strictly in a 12-bar blues song.

Lick 6, derived mostly from the minor pentatonic scale, makes use of an F9/F6 combination (discussed thoroughly in *More Blues You Can Use*) in the first bar. This firmly establishes that you are on the IV chord before moving back to the I chord in the third bar of the lick.

Lick 7 also comes from the minor pentatonic scale. While it is a two-bar figure, either half stands on its own quite well and can be used anywhere you have the IV chord.

Lick 8 makes use of both the major and minor pentatonic scales. Play the F major and F9 chords given in the music to see how the notes of the lick come from those chords.

At this point in the progression (bars 7 and 8), we reach a two-bar stretch of the I chord. The following licks can be played there. You will recall that the I chord is played in bars 3 and 4. These licks will fit there, and any licks from bars 3 and 4 can be played in bars 7 and 8 as well.

Lick 9 is mostly made from the major pentatonic, until the change to the V (or IV) chord is anticipated at the end of the second bar. Then it switches over to the minor. (Note: the last bar is played over a IV chord instead of the V chord found in bar 9. You'll have to omit or change this bar if you use it in that part of the progression.)

Licks 10 and *11* are built from the minor pentatonic scale. Notice how the last four notes of *Lick 11* flow into the V9 chord at the end. You can use that little fragment of the lick to move to a V chord anywhere in a tune.

Lick 10

Lick 11

Now we are at the last four bars of the blues progression. In bar 9, you play on a V chord and move to a IV chord in bar 10. Bars 11 and 12 make up the *turnaround* bars of the tune. In this progression, we are using the I-IV-I-V turnaround—the most common one found in the blues today.

Licks 12 and *13* both start with a one-beat pickup in bar 9 and move through the V to the IV chord in the next bar. Both also end on the first beat of the turnaround. That note can be changed to fit a stock turnaround lick if you want to use one there. In *Lick 12,* the notes in the first bar are derived from the G minor pentatonic scale—that of the V chord! That's OK; it works (as you will hear). Then you move to the C minor pentatonic scale to play over the IV chord and finish off the lick.

Lick 13 begins with notes from the G9 chord, followed by a fragment from the C minor pentatonic scale to lead into the IV chord. You could insert another lick or motive in the last three beats of the lick before the turnaround.

Lick 14 is longer and is played through to the end of the turnaround. Again, the notes played over the V chord are from the G (V) minor pentatonic scale. The rest of the lick is from the C minor pentatonic scale.

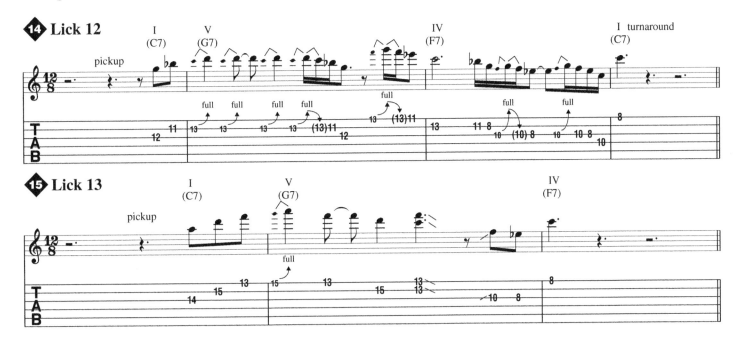

Lick 12

Lick 13

Lick 14

While *Lick 14* took us through the end of the progression, *Licks 12* and *13* brought us right up to the turnaround. Now we need a lick to finish off the tune; the last lick in this section will do just that.

Lick 15 starts off with the first five notes spelling a C7 chord. Look at the chord grid above the music to see where they come from. You'll find that chord tones are very effective in lead playing, especially when the chord changes are faster (as they are in this turnaround). Next, you play the C minor pentatonic until you get to the end, where you play a G7 arpeggio in the last two beats of the last bar.

Lick 15

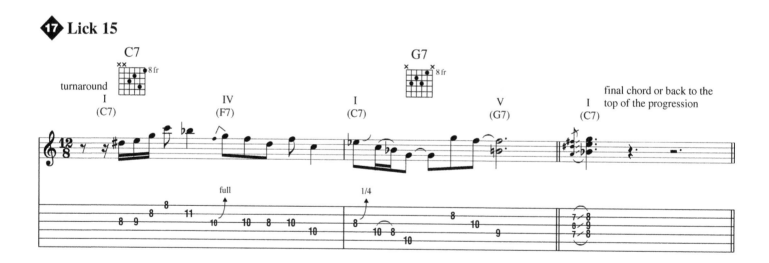

Before we move on to the next section, let's take a look at how you can put these licks together to build a solo. It's a fairly simple task. You just pick what you like and place it within the proper bars of the tune. You have to be sure to begin the licks on the correct beat. For example, *Lick 1* begins on beat two of the first bar. If you start it on any other beat (beat one, for example), you'll be off later on in the lick. That is not to say that you'll necessarily be wrong; the lick might fit just fine with some small adjustments later in the phrase to keep up with the chord changes. Nonetheless, you have to be aware of any adjustments you are making.

For the solo we're building with the licks in this chapter, we'll start off with *Lick 1*. This will take us through the first four bars of the tune. There is a short rest at the end of the lick. That will give us time to get to the next lick, which will be *Lick 8*.

Notice that *Lick 8* begins with a one-beat, three-note pickup in bar four of the tune. *Lick 1* doesn't leave enough room for the pickup, so we'll just leave it out. You can do that as long as it sounds complete to you. I think it works just fine.

We are now at bar 7, where the tune returns to the I chord for two bars. Looking through the licks that will fit over the next two bars, we find *Lick 10* fits well here. Since the last lick actually runs into the first beat of bar 6, we have to decide whether to shorten the first note of *Lick 10* or shave off the last three notes of *Lick 8*—the ones that extend into bar 6. After playing it both ways, I decided that it sounds best to shorten *Lick 8*. You may decide to alter *Lick 10* instead, and you'd be as right as I am. Either way works, so it's simply a matter of taste as to which way you choose to go.

We're at bars 8 and 9 now, and we need a lick to play over the V-IV chord movement. I like *Lick 14* here, and it takes us all the way through the turnaround. At this point you can either take a second chorus, or the vocals, or another soloist can start their thing here.

The next page has the solo written out for you to look at.

PUTTIN' THE PIECES TOGETHER
12-bar Blues in the Key of C

The process that we went through above takes place in an instant when you are actually playing. You have to make those decisions as the solo is progressing. If you know the licks well enough, you can grab them in the blink of an eye.

As you work through these licks, putting them together to make a larger chunk of a solo, experiment with their position in the tune to see what works and what doesn't. Take your time working with them and altering them. And don't forget to transpose the licks to all of the other keys. You'll end up with new licks based on the old ones, increasing the size of your "bag" of licks! You'll also get a much better understanding of how they work with the different chords.

SECTION 2

UP-TEMPO BOUNCE: LICKS 16 - 30

Swingin' Licks for a Shuffle in A

This section gives you a lot of licks that can be used in a blues shuffle. You will recall that a shuffle has a *triplet feel* where the eighth notes *swing*. In this style, the second eighth note of the beat is delayed slightly, the first one having "borrowed" some of its time. The downbeat, however, is steady and constant. If you think of the beat as being divided into three smaller, even beats (triplets), you can work out the rhythm of a shuffle. The first eighth note gets two of the triplet beats and the second eighth note gets one.

Basic count: 1   2   3   4
Eighth notes: (one-and) (a) (two-and) (a) (three-and) (a) (four-and) (a)

If this is confusing, listen to the audio for this section and for Section 5—especially the rhythm section (full band) recordings (tracks 79 and 82). If that doesn't help, there is a detailed discussion of shuffle-type swing in *Blues You Can Use*, p.19.

Here's the chord progression in the key of A, played by the band on audio track 79.

🔷79 Shuffle Progression in A

Up-tempo with a Swing Feel

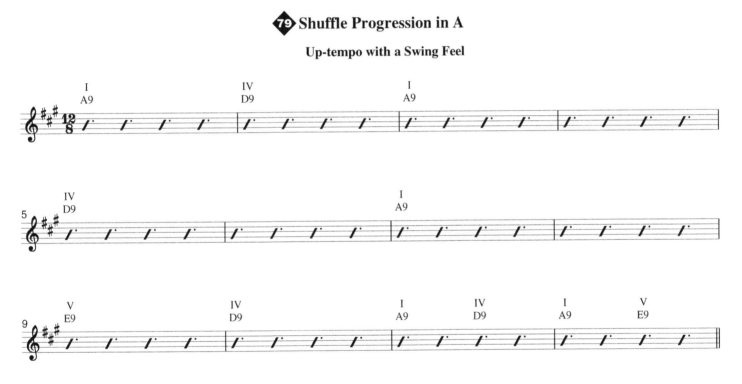

Now for the licks.

Lick 16 is played through the opening four bars of the progression. It has a short pickup, which is played either in a special "pickup measure" in the very beginning of the tune, or at the end of bar 12 in a previous chorus. *Lick 16* is made up of notes from the A major (in the pickup) and minor pentatonic scales (in the second full bar). It ends with a slide into the root and 3rd of the A chord, and then moves down to the ♭7th and 9th of the chord. The chordal notes are used as a sort of punctuation—very effective.

Lick 17 is nearly identical to *Lick 16,* with some changes in the notes. Most importantly, on the IV chord, you bend up a half-step to a C♮ instead of the C♯ as in *Lick 16.* The A9/A6 combination used in *Lick 6* is employed at the end. Again, the chord tones are used more as punctuation than as a melodic continuation of the lick.

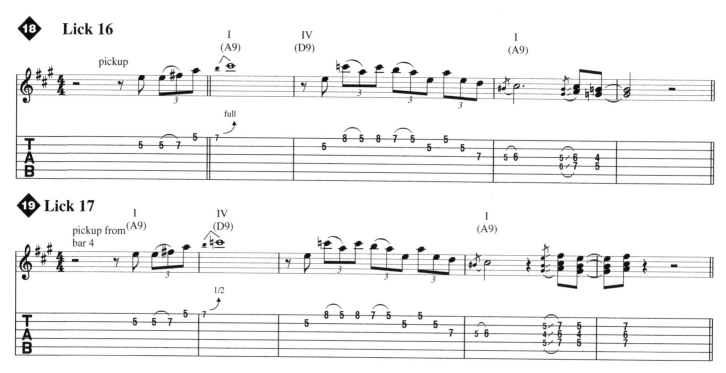

Licks 18 and *19* also run through the first four bars of the progression. *Lick 18,* made up of notes from the minor pentatonic scale, ends with the 3rd and ♭7th of the I chord. They are the essential notes of a seventh chord (explained thoroughly in *Blues You Can Use Guitar Chords). Lick 19* begins with double stops, hammering on to the 5th and ♭7th of the I chord. It continues with notes from the major pentatonic scale over the IV chord and ends with a slide into the 3rd and 5th of A7 (C♯ and E) on the return to the I chord.

Lick 20, played over bars 1 - 5, comes entirely from the minor pentatonic scale until the end, where it slides into the 3rd, 5th and ♭7th of the IV (D) chord. Notice how the basic motive is repeated in different positions on the neck. You get a different feel in each position and the surrounding notes are different, making for different possibilities in your choice of the next licks. This lick can be played over four straight bars of a I chord, as you sometimes find in the opening of a blues tune.

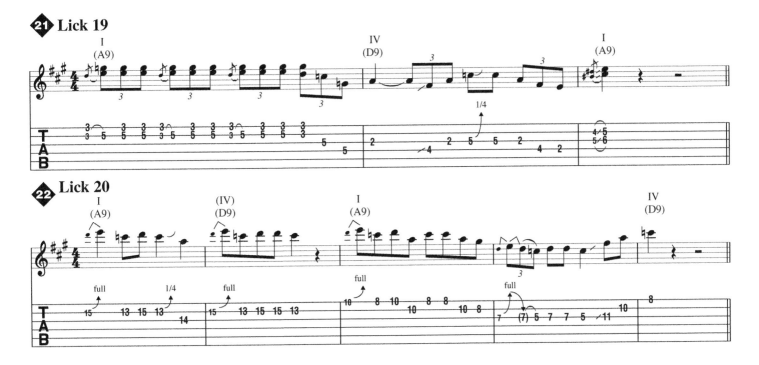

Lick 19

Lick 20

Lick 21 begins in bar 3 on the I chord, extends through the change to the IV chord in bars 5 and 6, and ends back on the I chord in bar 7. Notice the slight change in the first four bars—from an E♮, which is the 5th of the I chord, to E♭, which is the ♭9 of the IV chord. It's pretty dissonant, creating a lot of tension, but the tension is released when you return to E♮ in bar 7.

Lick 22 makes use of notes from both the major and minor pentatonic scales. Notice that a C♯ is used on the I chord and a C♮ is used over a IV chord, giving a strong sense of the chord change.

Another lick that can be played in the same part of the tune, *Lick 23* also makes use of the switch between C♯ and C♮ on the I and IV chords, respectively. It also slides into a I chord at the change in bar 7—this time a partial A7 (the 3rd – C♯, and ♭7th - G) from one fret below.

Lick 24 starts out with the notes of the IV7 chord (D, F♯, A, and C) and then changes to the notes of the minor pentatonic scale with the addition of a C♯. It ends on an E and D—the root and ♭7th of the V chord (E).

Lick 21

Lick 25 plays around with a variation of the E♭ to E♮ thing that we saw in *Lick 20*. You can use that figure over a IV chord wherever it occurs in a tune. The rest of the notes come from the A minor pentatonic scale. *Lick 25* can be used in bars 5-8.

The next two licks, *Lick 26* and *Lick 27*, fit in bars 5–8. Both start right on the IV chord without a pickup from the previous bar. They are both made up of notes from the A minor pentatonic scale on the IV chord, and make use of the C♯ when they get back to the I chord.

27 Lick 25

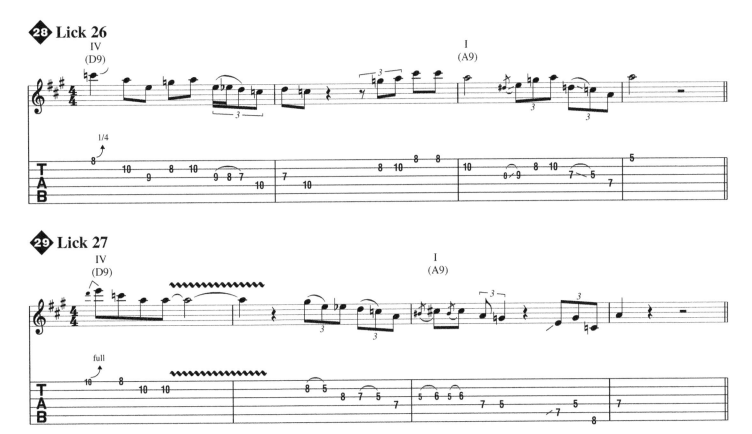

28 Lick 26

29 Lick 27

The last group of licks brought us to bar 9, where the V chord first appears in the progression, then to the IV chord in bar 10, and finally to the turnaround in bars 11 and 12. That's where this final group of licks picks up.

Lick 28 is made up of motives that, by themselves, can be smaller licks. The first lick in bar 9 on the V chord gets its notes from the major pentatonic scale. In the next bar is a lick that can be used any place the IV chord appears. It can even be extended to two bars to fit over bars 5 and 6. The last two bars (the turnaround) contain the classic descending chromatic line from the root (A) down to the 5th (E).

Lick 29 starts out with double stops consisting of the root, ♭7th, and 5th of the I chord (A). It changes to the major pentatonic when you reach the IV chord in bar 10. In the turnaround, there is a return to the minor pentatonic, with a C♯ on the I chord. You can see how important this little device (C♯ to C♮ switch) is.

Lick 30 is a turnaround lick. It starts with an A chord (C♯-E-A) and then moves down through a short minor pentatonic scale run to the root of the V chord (E).

Lick 28

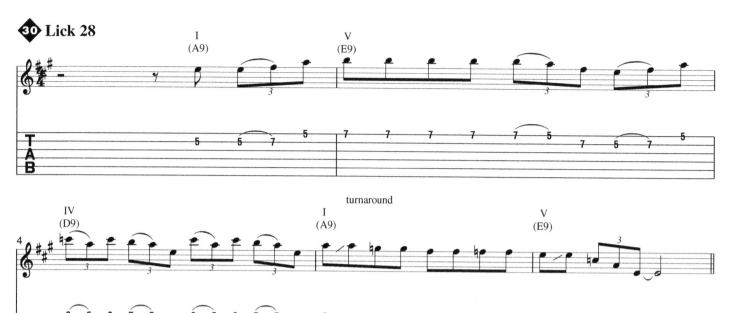

Lick 29

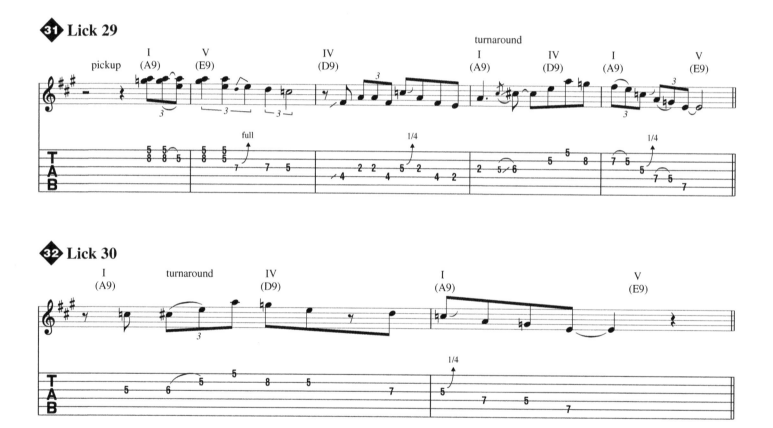

Lick 30

Remember to work through all of the licks in all keys. Change them around, fiddle with them, and make new ones.

SECTION 3

ROCKIN' IT UP: LICKS 31- 45

Hot Blues-Rock Licks in the Key of E

Now let's turn our attention to another style—blues-rock. It's generally an up-tempo style of music that's great for dancing and a whole lot of fun! There are lots of flashy, rapid licks, full of lots of notes. While they often seem incredibly complex and difficult when you first hear them, you'll see in this section that, on closer examination, many of them are simple and straightforward— though not all of them are. They do go by fast, and you will need to develop a rapid picking technique if you haven't already. In fact, just learning and playing these licks will help you develop speed in your playing.

The licks in this section are written in the key of E and they often make use of open strings. Some of the open-string licks will be difficult to transpose to other keys, but it is worth the effort to try. You'll find that since E is the guitar key with the most open strings, it is perfect for this style. It contains the lowest, biggest sounding note on the instrument for the root of the key, and there are lots of quick licks that lend themselves to the open position on the guitar. Transposing from this key will change the feel and the sound more than changing from any other key.

Most of the licks you use in slower blues tunes and in shuffles can be used in an up-tempo blues-rock style tune: all you do is speed them up. Some are more closely associated with this style, and the licks included in this section are among those.

The chord progression we'll use is only slightly different from the ones we've seen so far. The only change is that it does not change to the IV chord in bar 2. Instead, it stays on a I chord for the first four bars of the tune, and then you change to the IV chord just as you did in the previous progressions. In the last two bars of the tune you just stay on the I chord. Here it is written out:

80 Rockin' Blues Progression

12-bar Blues-rock Progression in E

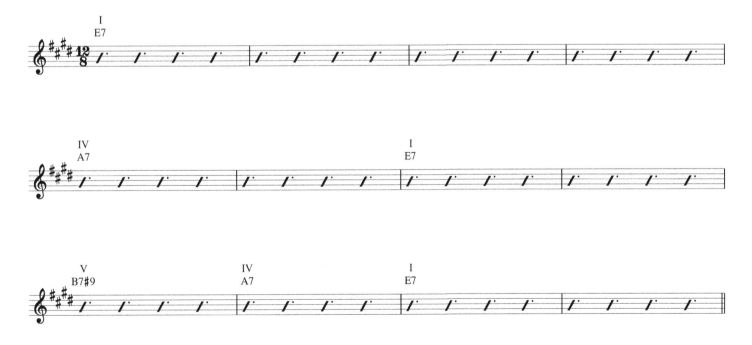

The first three licks are actually variations of the same two-bar lick. All three variations begin alike on the I chord, and only change in that last half. How they end depends on the chord on which you are ending. The first, *Lick 31*, stays on a I chord. *Lick 32* ends on a IV chord and *Lick 33* ends on a V chord. All three are built from an E blues scale. They can be used anywhere there is a I chord in the tune as long as you use the ending that corresponds to the ending chord.

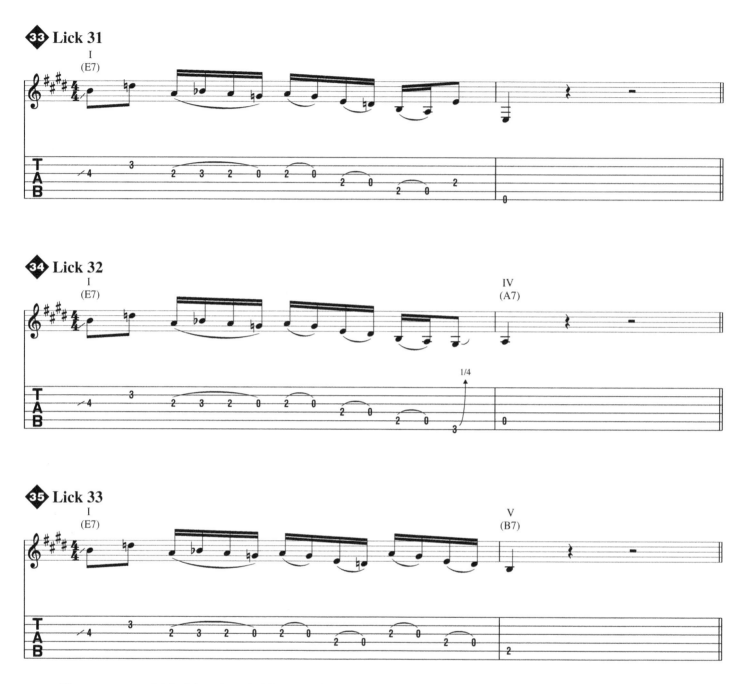

The next two, *Lick 34* and *Lick 35,* are built from the E minor pentatonic scale.

Lick 34, fingered in the twelfth position, includes a G♯, the 3rd of the I chord (E), and is played either in the opening four bars of the progression, or in the two-bar stretch of the I chord beginning in bar 7. It can also be played an octave lower using open strings. Try it both ways.

Lick 35 can be played in the opening four bars of the tune or over the change to the IV chord, with the pickup in bar 4. Like most of the open-position licks in this section, it can be played up an octave at the twelfth fret.

Also played in the first four bars of the blues-rock chord progression, *Lick 36* and *Lick 37* are found at the twelfth fret. As with the above licks, they can be played an octave lower at the nut.

Lick 36 makes use of double stops with notes primarily from the E minor pentatonic scale. *Lick 37* also has double stops, taking the notes from a combination of the E major pentatonic and blues scale. It is reminiscent of the '50's blues-rockers, and you should spend a lot of time playing and changing around these double stops; transpose them to all keys. They are really very important to the blues-rock style.

36 Lick 34

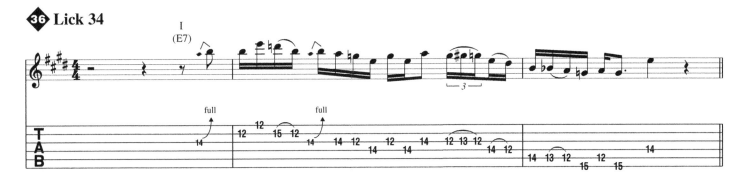

37 Lick 35

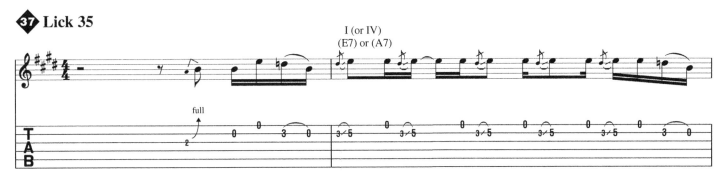

38 Lick 36

39 Lick 37

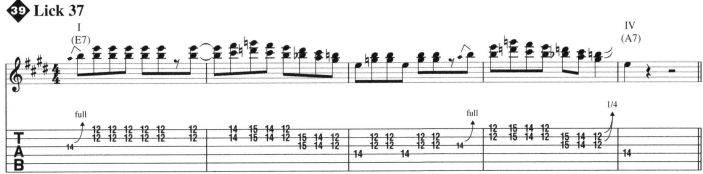

Here are some more licks with double stops. This time the double stops are taken from the notes of the chord over which you are playing.

Lick 38 makes heavy use of double stops. Begin with the root and 5th of the E chord and slide first into the 3rd and 5th, and then the ♭7th and 3rd of the E7 chord. In the third bar of the lick, you change to the IV chord and slide into the 3rd and ♭7th, 3rd and 5th, and ♭7th and 3rd of the A7 chord. The lick ends on an E—the root of the I chord. It really moves along the neck—all the way from the twelfth position down to the nut. You can see that a good knowledge of chord construction is essential to developing and understanding this type of lick.

Lick 39 is played on the change from the I to the IV chord, with the half-beat pickup in bar 3. The three-note chords played over the IV chord are partial A7♭9 chords. Be sure and transpose this one playing over the I and IV chords in every key.

Lick 40 is pure flash and comes from the minor pentatonic scale.

The next two licks begin at bar 5, where the chord progression has moved to a IV chord.

Lick 41 starts on a C♯ (the 3rd of the IV chord, A), and moves through the root, 5th, and back to the root in the first four notes. Following a descending run made up of notes from the E minor pentatonic scale with the addition of a C♯, you get to the second bar of the lick which contains the root, 5th, and ♭7th of the chord, and a slide up on a double stop to the ♭7th and 3rd of the A7 chord. The lick ends with a long, one-position run through the minor pentatonic scale played over the I chord.

Lick 42 makes use of the chord tones used in *Lick 41,* and ends with a fast and flashy run down to a B—the root of the V chord. Played at the nut, the run sounds difficult but it's not really that tough; master this one and you'll really impress your friends.

43 Lick 41

44 Lick 42

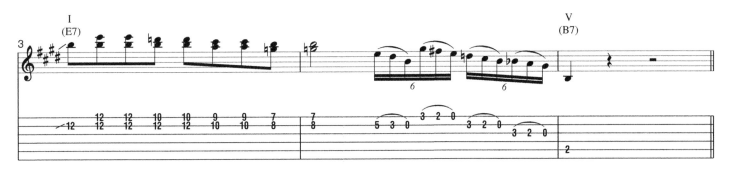

The next three licks take us from the V chord in bar 9, back to the I chord, and then to the end of the tune.

Lick 43 makes use of double stops that are very similar to those found in *Licks 36* and *37*. However, they fit over the V chord here and are played in the seventh position. In the second bar of the lick, there are one-fret slides up to the ♭7th (D) and 3rd (G-sharp) of the E7 (V) chord. Then it moves through an easy minor-pentatonic run down to the open low E.

Lick 44 also uses double stops on the V chord, creating quite a bit of tension and dissonance. The lick ends with a little open-string flash on the I chord.

Lick 45 actually starts in bar 10, though you could start it a bar earlier repeating the motive found there. It ends on an E, the root of the I chord. Very often in the blues-rock style, a chorus ends on the root of the I chord. There are exceptions, though, and when you avoid ending the turnaround on the root, you can create a sense that the solo is going on for another 12 bars.

45 Lick 43

46 Lick 44

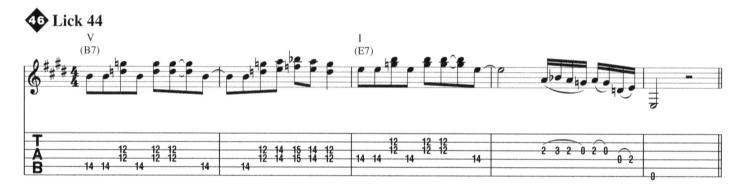

47 Lick 45

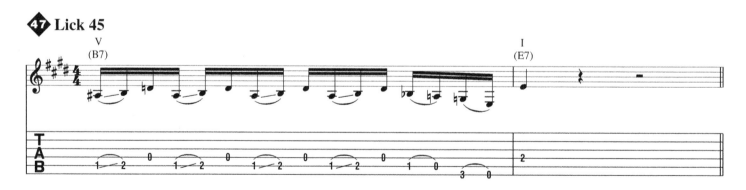

As I pointed out earlier, the open-string licks are often quite difficult to transpose, but see what you can do—you might be surprised by what you can come up with.

SECTION 4

A BIT OF FLASH: LICKS 46 - 60

Impressive Licks in a Slow Blues in G

This section contains more slow blues licks—this time with a little bit more flash. Instead of basic, simple licks, these make use of a lot more notes in the same amount of time! The licks in this section are difficult; practice small segments of them at first. It's worth the effort because they are exciting and a whole lot of fun to play.

You should have a pretty good idea of how to use the licks at this point. Rather than go into detail about where they can be played in the tune, I'll leave it up to you to work it out. The chords are still given in the music, so you shouldn't have any problem. They are given here in no particular order so that you can figure out where to put them in the 12-bar blues progression. They are written in the key of G. The following 12-bar quick-change progression can be heard on track 81.

81 Another Slow Blues
12-bar Blues Progression in G

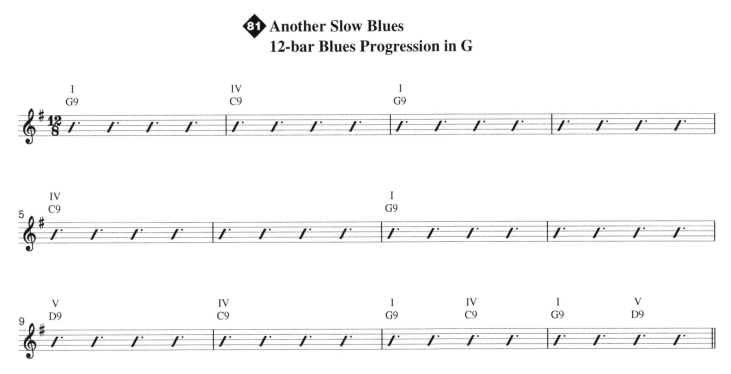

You should also be able to analyze the licks with some ease now. They are no more complicated than any of the previous licks, even though they generally contain more notes.

Licks 46 and *47* are both derived from the minor pentatonic scale. *Lick 46* is a turnaround lick ending on a D7#9 chord for the final V chord. *Lick 47* gets its notes from a C9 chord on the change to the IV.

48 Lick 46

27

49 ▶ Lick 47

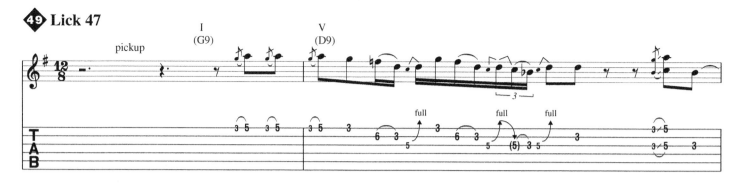

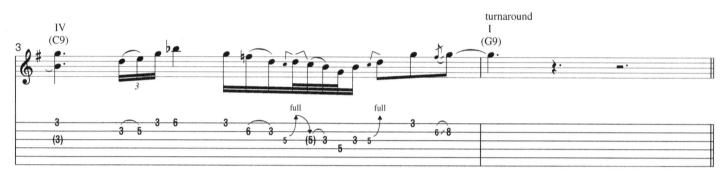

The next four licks *(48-51)* are built from the G blues scale. They can be tricky to play because of the rhythm, and because everything goes by very quickly. Take your time and learn them slowly at first, gradually building up speed. *Lick 50* can be used as a fill lick between lines of the vocal verses.

50 ▶ Lick 48

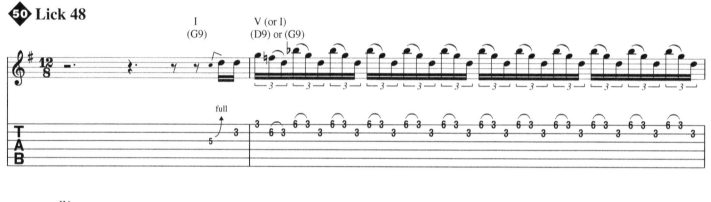

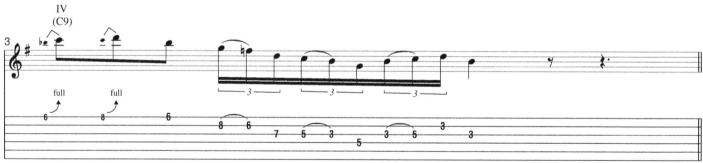

51 Lick 49

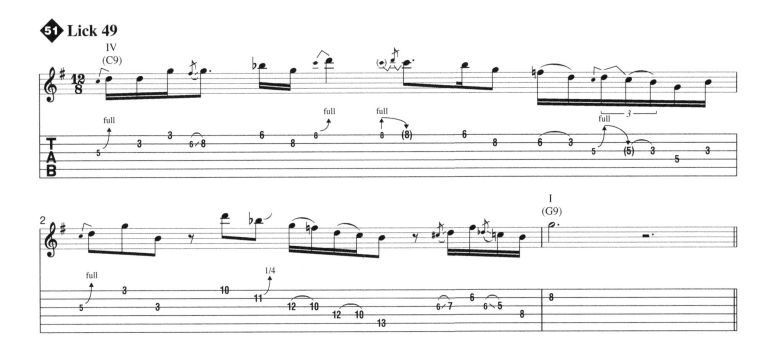

52 Lick 50

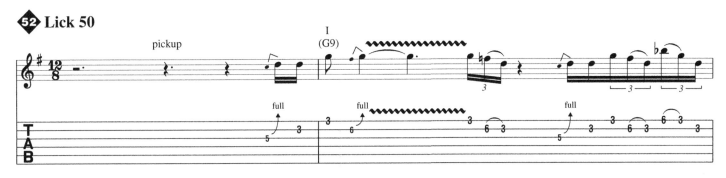

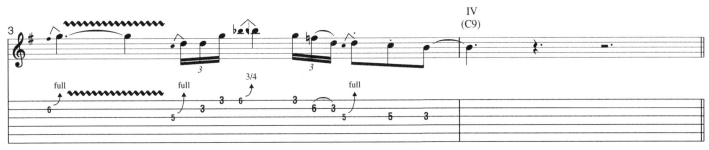

53 Lick 51

Licks 52 and *53* are both made up of repeated patterns. When you repeat a pattern like this, it's called a *sequence*. The patterns are marked in the music. Many fancy licks are created this way. You could extend either lick by repeating the sequence for another bar.

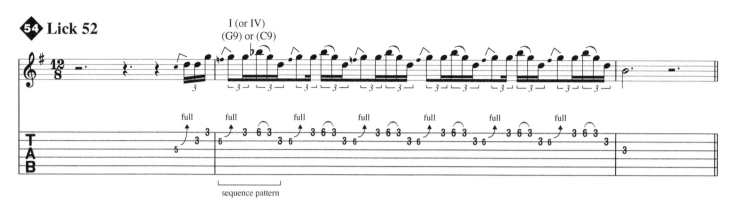

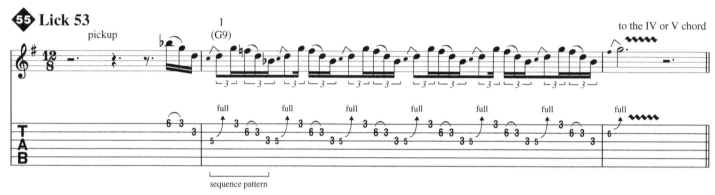

Licks 54 and *55* also make use of sequences. *Lick 54* has a double-stop lick repeated over the IV chord that is similar to those found in the last section. *Lick 55* starts out with a sequence repeated at different positions and pitches. In the second bar, there is another sequence, and the lick finally closes with figures from the G blues scale.

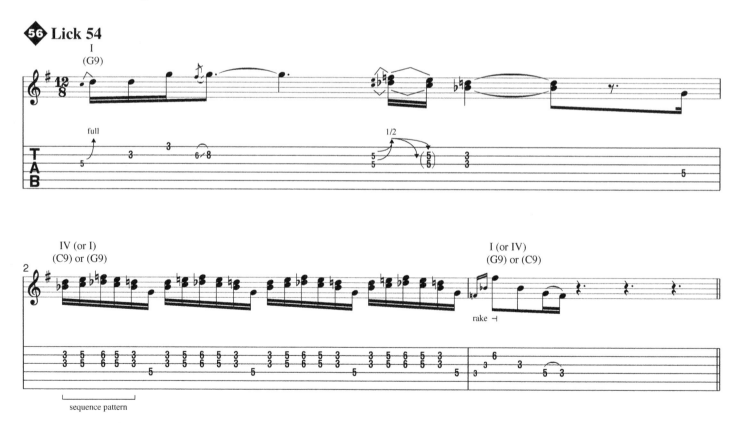

57 **Lick 55**

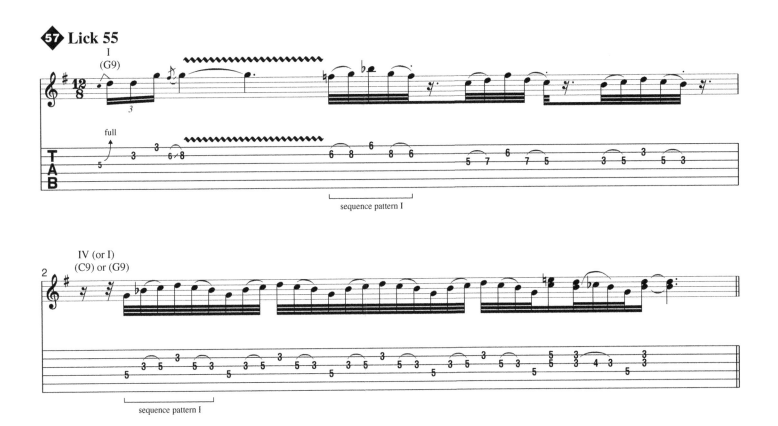

After a short pick-up, *Lick 56* stresses an A, the 5th of the V chord (D9), before moving on to quick blues-scale figures through the IV and I chords and the beginning of the turnaround. *Lick 57* is pure blues-scale flash over the same chords.

58 **Lick 56**

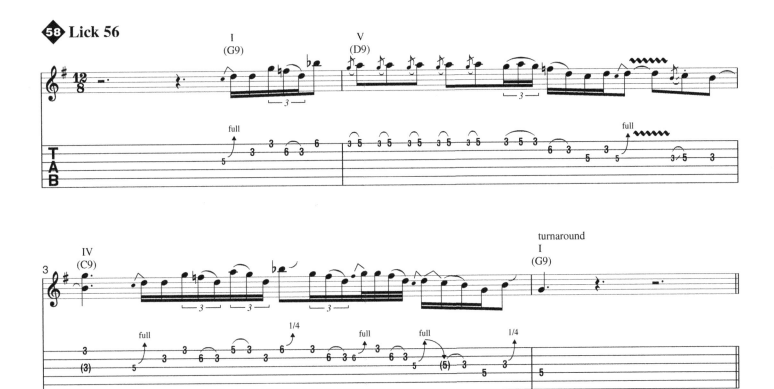

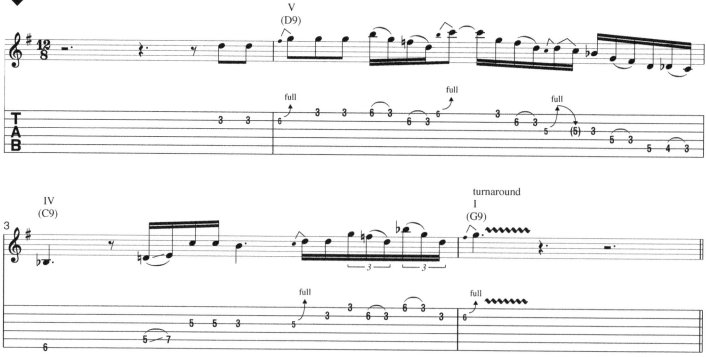

Lick 58 is a turnaround lick which repeats the short motive in the beginning two more times with some variation. Notice the slide up from a B♭ to a D at the tenth fret and the immediate return to the B♭ at the third fret. This is tricky, and will most likely take some practice to get down.

Lick 59 moves around the fingerboard a bit, through different patterns of the blues scale, and finally arrives at a sequence at the end. The string rake at the beginning of the repeat should be played hard, making a strong accent on the first note of the sequence and creating a powerful ending to the lick.

In the final lick of this section, Lick 60, we have another sequence. On the last repeat, it's altered in a way that speeds up the rhythm and gives a sense of motion towards the end of the lick. The motion slows down as you reach the slide into the I9 chord at the end.

60 Lick 58

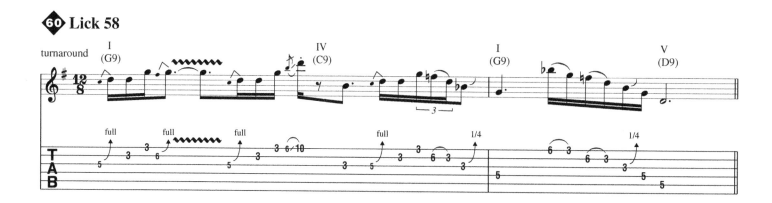

Lick 59

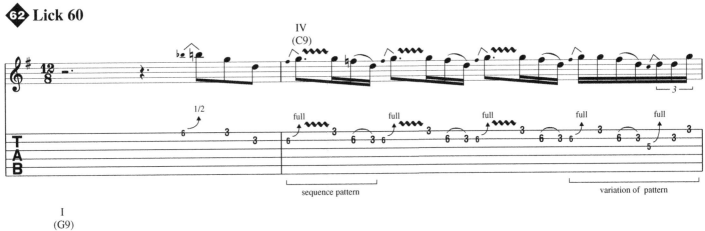

Lick 60

SECTION 5

A TASTE OF JAZZ: LICKS 61 - 75

Jazzy Licks and a Shuffle in F

The blues has spawned a great many styles of music over the past century or so, from rock 'n' roll and rhythm & blues to jazz and pop. Once those styles have become firmly established with characteristic licks of their own, they often find their way back to the blues with an infusion of new ideas. This leads to the evolution of the blues.

We've seen some examples of the blues-rock style, and now, for the final section of this book, we'll look at some jazz-style blues licks. They very often are formed from the chords more than from the blues or pentatonic scales.

As with the last section, the licks are not in any particular order. You'll see by the chord symbols in the music where they fit in the chord progression. Remember that, for the most part, the licks in a shuffle are played with a strong swing feel.

The chord progression we'll be using for these licks is a quick-change shuffle in the key of F. You can hear it on audio track 82. Here it is:

82 12-bar Shuffle in F

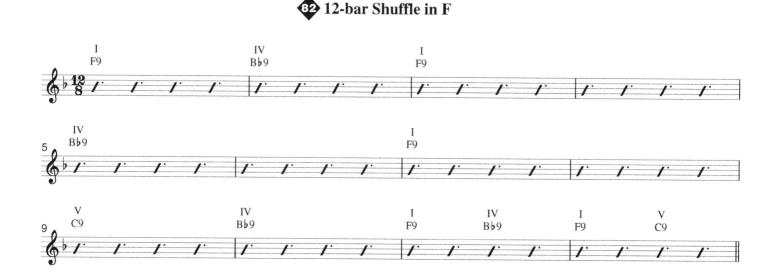

Lick 61, the first of the licks in this section, is played over a I chord. It gets most of its notes from the F blues scale until the end. There, you slide up one fret to the ♭7th and 3rd of the F7 (I) chord. At the very end, you slide back down one fret to the 3rd and ♭7th of the B♭7 chord (IV). Notice how the lower note (E♭), the ♭7th of the I chord, moves down to a D, the 3rd of the IV chord. At the same time, the 3rd of the I chord (A) slides down to A♭ to become the ♭7th of the IV chord. This lick could be used as a short ending lick if you stop on the E♭/A double-stop at the asterisk in measure 2.

Lick 62 is a cool lick with notes from both the F major pentatonic and blues scale.

Lick 63 is played high up the neck in the thirteenth position, and is derived primarily from the minor pentatonic scale.

Lick 61

Lick 62

Lick 63

The next three licks get most of their notes from the minor pentatonic scale. At the end of *Lick 64*, the notes are from an F7 chord. The phrase begins with the 3rd in the beginning of the fourth bar of the lick, moves on to the root and 3rd, then finally down to the ♭7th and 9th of the chord.

While *Lick 65* is all minor pentatonic, *Lick 66* takes some of its notes from the F major pentatonic and blues scales.

Lick 64

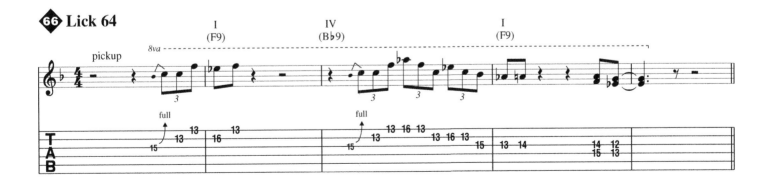

With bends on unusual notes, *Lick 67* follows the V to IV progression nicely before returning to a blues-scale figure.

Lick 68 takes its notes in the first two bars from a Bb13 chord, and from an F7 chord in the third and fourth bars. The chord tones are given in the music. You can find the notes in the chord diagrams above the music.

Lick 69 is derived primarily from the F blues scale.

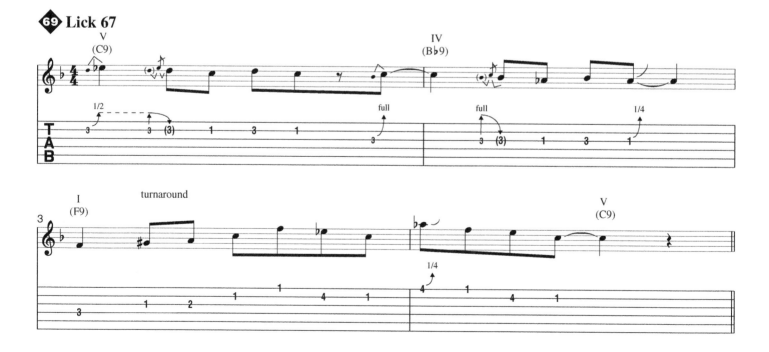

After repeating a tenth-position figure from the major pentatonic scale in *Lick 70,* you leap down to the first-position finish with a string rake and a figure ending on the 3rd of the I chord.

Lick 71 begins with a repeated bent double stop and moves down through the minor pentatonic scale to the 3rd of the I chord.

Lick 72 makes use of a sequence played on the I and IV chords, and then moves through a major sounding run (using the F Mixolydian mode—given in the introduction) to the 3rd (D) and root (B♭) of the IV chord.

72 **Lick 70**

73 **Lick 71**

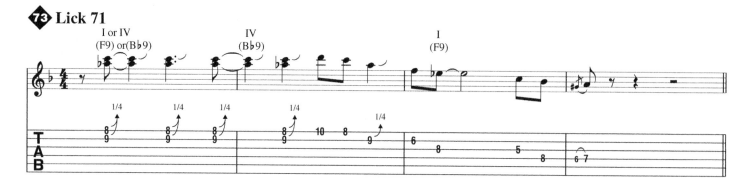

74 **Lick 72**

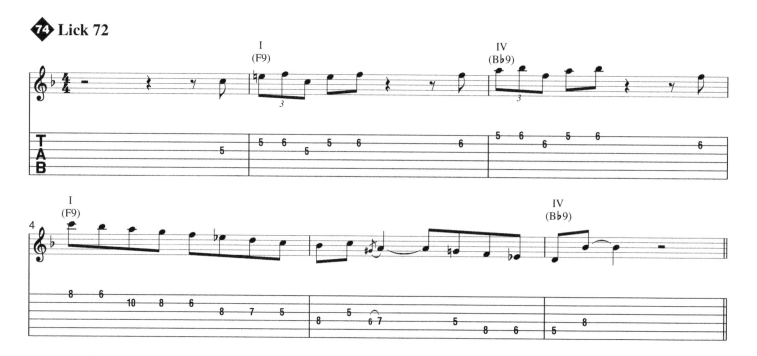

Lick 73 starts with notes from the minor pentatonic scale. The change to the I chord in the third bar of the lick outlines an F minor chord, which creates dissonance when played over an F7 chord. That's because the F minor chord has a D♯ (a bluesy sound) and the F7 contains a D♯. Try playing them together (third string, seventh fret and second string, fourth fret) to hear the source of the dissonance. The lick is then mixed with notes from the major pentatonic when you reach the V chord, and it moves back to the minor pentatonic at the end.

Lick 74 starts out with an F minor pentatonic scale which changes to an F blues scale on the I chord.

The final lick of the book, *Lick 75*, has a chromatic figure used in a sequence—first on the I chord and then the IV chord. The lick ends on a IV-I motive, created by changing the lower note from B♭ (the root of the IV chord) down to A (the 3rd of the I chord). The upper note (F), which doesn't change, is the 5th of the IV chord and the root of the I.

75 Lick 73

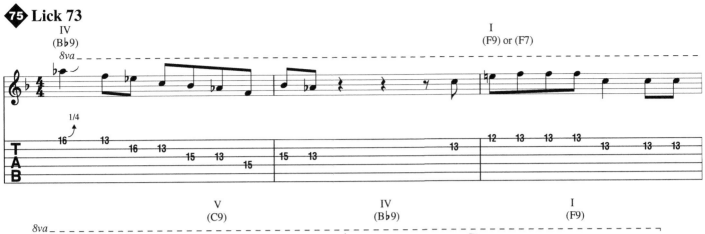

76 Lick 74

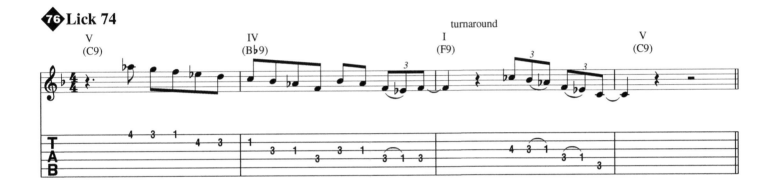

77 Lick 75

WHERE TO GO FROM HERE

Suggestions for Continuing Your Studies

Now that you've finished this book and have played everything in every key and in every position on the guitar, you will probably want to move on to further studies. You may have a clear idea of what you want to do next, or you may not be sure. Whatever the case, you will want to have a somewhat organized approach if you don't want to waste a lot of time.

The first thing I would suggest is to listen to a lot of blues guitarists. Listen to the new (where the blues is headed) and the old (where it has come from). Listen to all styles. For starters, listen to Muddy Waters, John Lee Hooker, Albert King, B.B. King, Freddie King, T-Bone Walker, and Albert Collins. These are the essential players to study.

Also very important are Elmore James, Magic Sam, Otis Rush, Hubert Sumlin (Howlin' Wolf's guitar player), Johnny Winter, and Clarence "Gatemouth" Brown. Add to that list Stevie Ray Vaughan, Buddy Guy, and Jimi Hendrix (if you haven't already been listening to them).

These guitarists will give you a well-rounded education in the origins of electric blues—a sort of "Blues Guitar 101." The first group will give you a good start, but if you really want to learn the blues on your guitar, you need to listen to the other players mentioned above. There are more, but you can take your time discovering them after you've gone through the above.

Listen to them with your guitar in your hands as often as possible. Whenever you hear a lick you like, try to learn it right then and there. Play along. Pay close attention to the subtleties, like slight delays and their sense of time.

You should also learn basic harmony—how chords are built and how chord progressions work. You can learn it on your own, from a book (like my *Blues You Can Use Guitar Chords,* also from Hal Leonard), or with a teacher. A good teacher can make things a lot clearer and easier. A basic knowledge of chords and progressions will open up a whole world of possibilities to you. The two core books of this series—*Blues You Can Use* and *More Blues You Can Use*—will give you a good foundation in how to use that knowledge in your playing, with many examples and exercises.

Don't limit your listening to the blues. Listen to rhythm & blues recordings. Many of the great R&B players started with the blues, and the R&B style itself is an outgrowth of blues. Some important rhythm & blues guitar players are Curtis Mayfield, Cornell Dupree and Steve Cropper (from Booker T and the MGs and many more), to name just a few. Listen to jazz/blues/R&B crossover guitarists Sonny Sharrock and Lucky Peterson, too.

Listen to jazz as well. Some bluesy jazz guitarists include Kenny Burrell, Grant Green, George Benson (he crosses over to R&B as well), and my favorite, Wes Montgomery. They play jazz, but they have a lot of blues in their playing—with lots of blues licks.

Finally, play a lot! Play with friends. Seek out other musicians to jam with. They don't all have to be guitarists. Play with piano players, bassists, and horn players. Play with anyone who's interested in the blues. Look especially for players who are better than you—you'll learn more from them. Play at open jam sessions at your local night-clubs, if you can. Play as much as you can with anyone you find to keep up with you. Just be sure you have fun doing it!